The Lonely Little Christmas Tree

Written by Sonica Ellis

Illustrated by Harriet Rodis

ISBN 978-1-7372647-2-9

Dear Reader,

Just like the little tree in the story, things will get better. We just have to be patient. Great things take time. Until then, be kind to everyone you meet, because a little kindness can go a long way.

Happy holidays!

Love Always,

Sonnie

DEDICATION:

This book is dedicated to all the people who might be feeling lonely this holiday season. I will keep you in my prayers and put a special ornament on my tree for you. Stay warm.

The crisp December air was filled with festive cheer on the Christmas Tree Farm. Families hidden beneath layers of clothing walked tirelessly, all searching for the perfect tree.

When the day was done and the moon had woken
from its slumber, the trees huddled together.

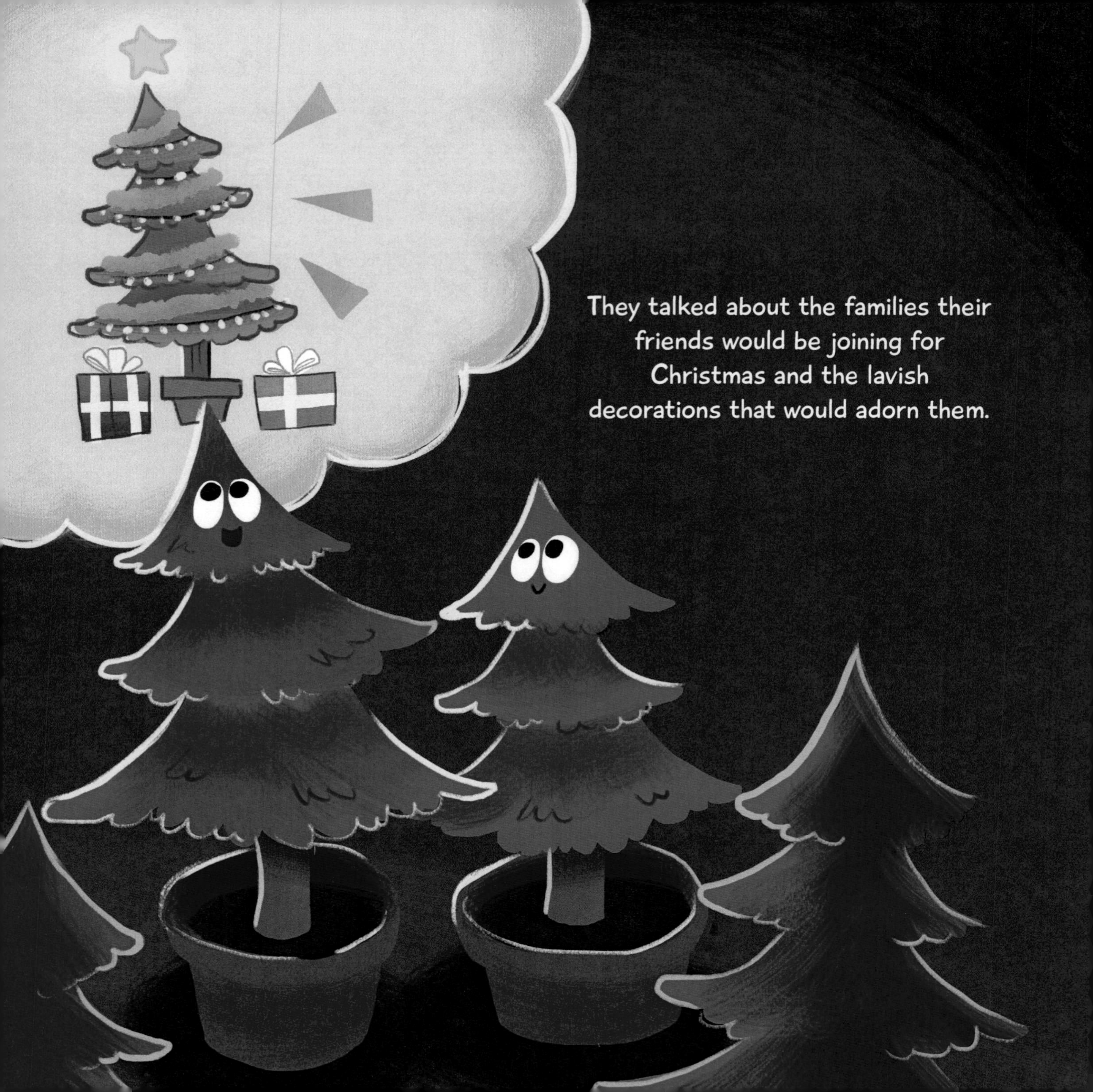

They talked about the families their friends would be joining for Christmas and the lavish decorations that would adorn them.

They wondered about the presents that would be placed at their feet and what the future had in store.

"I know I'll make a lucky family happy this Christmas," said Little Tree.
"I can hardly wait."

"You? Ha!" Leyland laughed.

"You!" another tree chuckled.
"What a funny little guy."

"You'll be lucky if you even get
picked," said Douglas.

"I'll get picked! Watch! You'll see!" shouted Little Tree so they could all hear him.

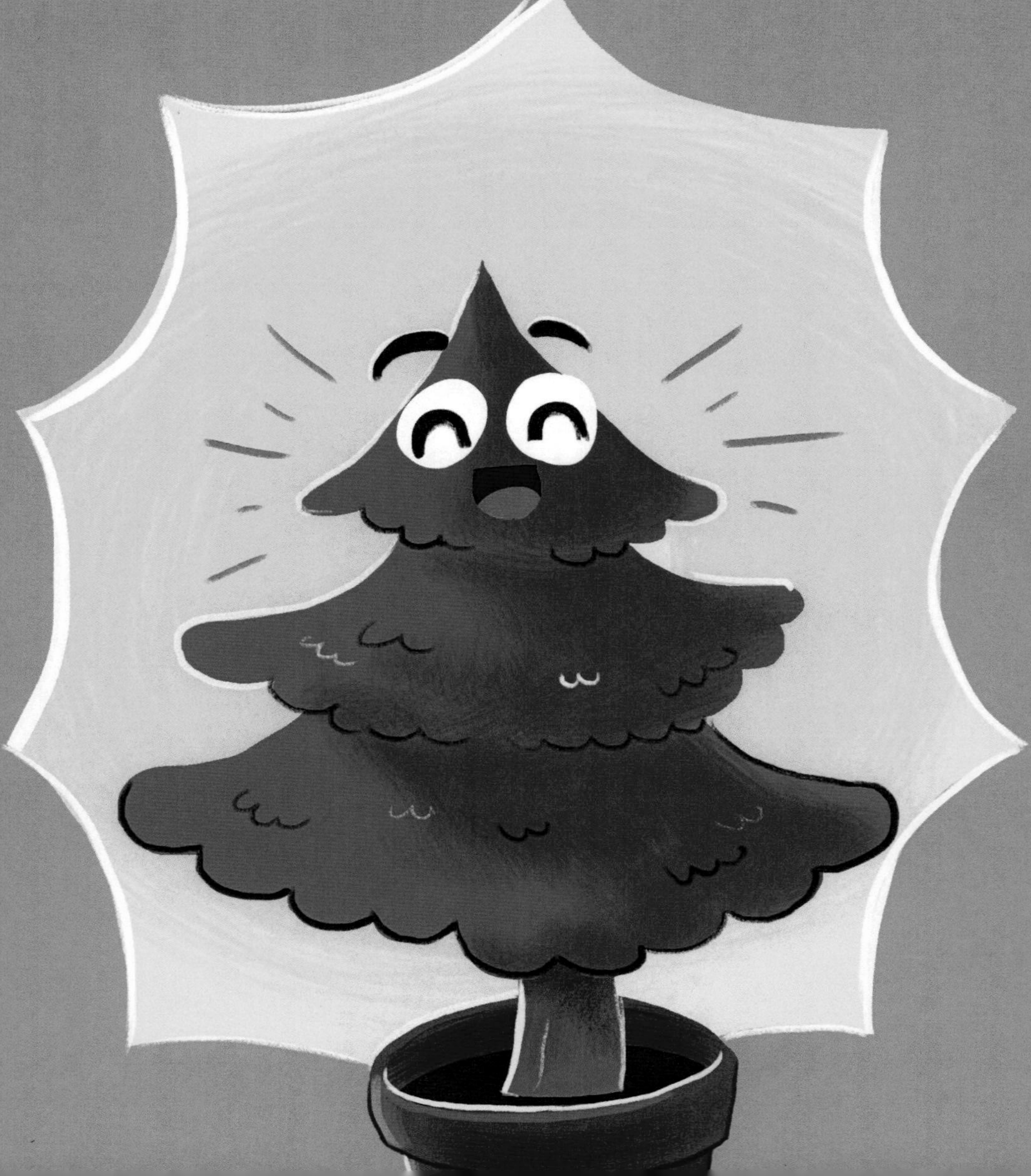

Every day a new family visited the Christmas Tree Farm, looking, touching, and smelling the trees. Kids played and laughed through the farm.
It was a great sight to behold.

Sadly, Little Tree didn't get picked.
He patiently waited.

"I see our little friend is still here," said Canaan, a slightly taller tree with rich green needles.

"I didn't get picked today, but I'm not losing hope. There's always tomorrow," replied Little Tree.

As the sun rose, visitors arrived at the farm and started picking trees.
Soon enough, a family wandered over to Little Tree.

"How about this one?" asked the man.

"It's too small. This one is more like it,"
replied the woman, pointing to another tree.

Before long, it was Christmas Eve, and Little Tree looked around and saw that he was all alone on the farm. He gave up all hope of being picked.

Dreams of having a family vanished from his thoughts.
He began doubting his worth and blaming himself.

Little Tree began to cry. "Maybe if I were perkier, stronger, or tall like the others, I would have been picked."

Suddenly, a mouse below interrupted him.
"Little Tree, don't you cry.
You're not alone.
Wait here. I'll be right back."

The mouse had an idea. She ran home and got some ornaments and told her neighbors what had happened.

It wasn't long before all the critters at the Christmas Tree Farm had heard about Little Tree's dilemma. Each brought an ornament or a present to place at Little Tree's feet.

Soon Little Tree was dressed in lights and ornaments, and a star was placed on his head. He was surprised and touched by the animals' kindness.
He thanked them all.

"This is the best Christmas gift any tree could ask for!" Little Tree shouted. "Merry Christmas and goodnight!"

THE END

Let's start a Christmas tradition together for "The Lonely Little Christmas Tree."

Step 1: Draw!

Draw a picture of the Lonely Little Christmas tree, complete with Christmas decorations and beautifully wrapped gifts underneath. (Hint: Maybe mom and dad or grandma and grandpa want to help.)

Step 2: Tell!

Tell us about your tree. Does it have a name? What things are in the presents underneath? Do any of the ornaments have special meaning to you and your family?

Step 3: Share!

Like and follow our new Facebook page "The Little Christmas Tree Farm" and post your art, or email your drawings to Thelittlechristmastreefarm@yahoo.com and we will post it for you!

Made in United States
North Haven, CT
03 December 2022

27757623R00015